A gift from Rachel,
Hope you are well
— A Shalom Wilder

Under the Only Moon

Dwain Wilder

FootHills Publishing

Acknowledgements

Dying, and Squirrels, *Hot Air*, Vol 2
On Loma Garden, *Shadow Play*, Vol 3
The Dancing Bones of the Sea, *Shadow Play*, Vol 3
Dokusan, *Zen Bow*, 1988
Ghosts, *Lake Affect*, November, 2005
Grief's Terrain, Zen Bow, 2009; *Le Mot Juste*, 2007
A Small House, *Le Mot Juste*, 2008
The Fractal Roshi Explores the Bardo, *Zen Bow*, 2009
Pearl, *Le Mot Juste*, 2009
What Poetry Is, */Le Mot Juste/*, 2011
Last. Or Maybe First, /Zen Bow/, 2010-2011

Copyright © 2011 Dwain Wilder

Cover photo courtesy of the National Astronomical Observatory of Japan, © 2007

ISBN: 978-0-941053-31-0

FootHills Publishing
P.O. Box 68
Kanona, NY 14856
www.foothillspublishing.com

This book would have been impossible without the influences of my teachers, Roshi Phillip Kapleau and Roshi Bodhin Kjolhede. And in great measure Katherine Denison is also to be counted among teachers. Living with her, I have learned much in the joys and proprieties of intimacy and connectedness with all life.

I would also like to thank the members of the Rochester community of poets, many of whom give great thought and effort to bringing out the best in their fellow writers.

In particular, mention must be made of Kathryn Jospé, who offered many valuable notes on the poems and helped me clarify the trajectory, so to speak, of this book. Karla Linn Merrifield, dear friend and an extraordinary poet, volunteered to lend an editor's and proofreader's eye, pointing out instances where I didn't have the control of my materials that I thought, and making crucial poetic observations on the quality of a line here and there. And John Roche gave a final scrubbing to the manuscript, as well as other help.

Dwain Wilder
Rochester, NY
New Year's Day, 2011

Foreword

An old saying in Zen goes, "When a finger is pointing to the moon, don't examine the finger! Look at the moon." The moon has always been a symbol of the feminine, the hiddenness of the implicate order, to usurp David Bohm's phrase.[1] As the sun sheds light on matters of fact, so the moon's light glows in wisdom, implicating the ineffable.

The high task of poetry is to say something, concretely and simply, about the ineffabilities of the great matter of life and death. To do so, attention to the breath is important, for our connection to the ineffable is in the breath, wherein is grounded aspiration, inspiration, spirit, psyche.

So, in my view, poetry is not so much a visual artifact on the written page; rather it is a record of the poet's lived connection with those he loves, fellow Earthlings, the Earth itself, and the heavens and hells extending eternally, all around us. Poetry's tropes, forms and meters should reflect and recall, in some manner, the breathing body of that experience.

Some of the poems found here are an attempt to attend to that calling. Regarding these, I don't write as a discipline, but rather when something bites, cuts or delights. Other poems here have seemed to come out of some light-hearted moment, with no special merit other than a joy in expression.

And, lastly, comes a selection of short dedication verses that I inscribe inside the musical instruments I build for a living. These verses are often inspired by some scene I come upon while walking our dogs during the afternoons and evenings. These fellow Earthlings have called me out of doors and given me a wonderful opportunity to see the world more intimately, more broadly. I thank my wife and dear companion, Katherine Denison, for bringing them home. They're always an unexpected delight, even while rolling in fox pee.

Dwain Wilder

---

[1] David Bohm, *Wholeness And The Implicate Order*, 1980; London; Routledge

Dedication

To prisoners everywhere who, as do we all, yearn for liberation and seek it constantly according to our best light, to the best of our ability.

Table of Contents

FOREWORD	4
PRÉLUDE	9
What Poetry Is	9
The Fractal Roshi Explores the Bardo	10
The World and You, at Play	12
Home Roads	13
I. WHAT THE EYE KNOWS	14
The Dancing Bones of the Sea	14
In Praise of the Sea	15
Gill-over-the-ground	16
Magic Under	17
What the Eye Knows	19
Lacunae	20
Cajolery	21
II. HOME ROADS	22
Nested Dreams and Reasons	22
On Loma Garden	23
Daddy's Passing	25
Up Drop Jaw Hill	27
Labor Day	29
IV. LEARNING TO DIE	33
The Turtle of Running	33
Heat	34
Learning to Die in May	35
Your Mother's Last Breath	38
Mother's Day	39
Last. or Maybe First	40
My Hair	41
Dokusan	42
Unfinished Song	43
Grief's Terrain	44
Night Emergencies	45

V. You're Becoming a Song	46
Dreams with Katherine	46
A Small House	47
Regarding Roselle's Buddha,	48
Margaret Cried So, Our Last Night	49
Eve On Her Hill	50
You're Becoming a Song	51
Sassafras	53
Eve Gives Lavender	54
VI. Dulcimer Verses	55
Frog	55
Night Geese	56
First Love	57
Coffee	58
The Bell	59
The Use of Crying	60
Willow	61
Dukkha	62
Ghosts	63
Night Song	64
Canon	65
Autumn	66
Moon	67
Me	68
Wolf's Moon	69
Spring Vigil	70
Samadhi	71
April	72

Prélude

What Poetry Is

>, it must be some way
to find the silence
in the cracks and folds of things
that lets sound sing,
the vast silence
that beats on the hair in the ear
when a snowplow
hits the curb.

But sometimes it seems more like
the way the world rings with brilliance
when pain astonishes you,

bounces
scrapes
and skitters
across raw mind.

The Fractal Roshi Explores the Bardo

The fractal Roshi mounts the golden zafu facing the
    Buddha altar.
He lays aside his staff and draws toward himself the lectern,
    removes the top of his water cup
        (whose fair side recalls something,
        creating an impulse to
        filigree it onto the panels of the tan,
        slice it off the sides of the zendo's pillars,
        cut it into the edges of the windowpanes
        until the whole room swims in that curve)
    and sips, pauses,
launches into the Bardo,
    that transition
between life and death
    plentitude and sudden penury,
        where we confront the emptiness
        of the substantial.

Patterns fly from his lips as he speaks,
    bubbles containing bubbles
    forming arrays of semi-bubbles inside,
    nothingness outside.
Each boundary a perplexity of predicaments,
    quandary alternating with enigma,
    revealing surfaces of choices,
    pocked with instances of Void.

The fractal Roshi proceeds with odd, subtle logic,
    steers through momentary clouds
    of dilemma surrounding all change,
    urging alertness, attention,
    negotiating the Bardo.
    he is far from where he started
    yet not so far.

The fractal Roshi finishes, raises his cup,
    the upper curve of his lip matching.

His spine curves with the lectern's stave as he pushes it away,
akin to the swirls of his robe's skirts of as he gyres off the tan.
He prostrates before the Buddha
    who is there
    not there;
    Roshi and Buddha
Between not one,
    not two.

The World and You, at Play

It was I saw the seeming
    of the seesaw play while the wind
    sowed pebbles in our hair.
It was I had the caring of my brother's pet crow,
    stealing our bright pennies off to his night,
    as he haw-hawed summer till it flew away.

I broke the jars. I hid the treasure. I threw the stones.
I smelled the gravel where the cats all shat
    in the magic dark floor of the garage.
It was I saw Barry break his arm in a box,
    tumbling from the attic with his eyes shut bright.
What did he learn in the air?

It was I scarred the trees.
I wrecked the fences.
I fondled our hog's ears 'til butchering day.
The creeks full of crawdads
    swam with our cries where we
    found snake spit on the cockleburr shells,
    drowning in the torrents of the bottle-green skies
    when the dry spell broke that June.

I saw the seeming
    all the summer day
    green as the clover
    round as a knee
    dare of the eye
    brick of the shin
    deeps of the sewer trench
    hewn in the road.

It was I breathed the wish
It was I filled the fields
It was I lived to see
all our vast boy seeming
held in the heart
of the thunderhead throng
hovering on the edge of the world
and gone.

Home Roads

Out on the star prairies
the hydrogen clouds are everlasting
glowing darkly in the void
while the moon knits the mists
on the Arkansas fields
beside the home-bound road.

The day's road,
    Dharma's body taken for home, is blessed each day,
    the truckers' panicked black scrawls scrubbed
    from the stone each day, the fur and bone scraps
    burnished onto the stone each day
under the adamant sun.

The circadians scribble their ancient electric thrill
making the roadside woods and creeks their own in the night
and while the mists outlast the moon.

Just so, I make them all my own
while I reach for home.

I. What the Eye Knows

The Dancing Bones
of the Sea

While the moon practices the sea,
The beach and the bones of the sea,
The beach grinds its bones by the moon of the sea,
Dancing the dance of the bones of the sea.

When the moon practices the sea,
Combing the bones of the sea,
Quick is the light of the moon on the sea,
A figure for the dance of the bones in the sea.

When the sea practices bones,
While sea is sloughing its bones,
Patient are the beach's gestures of bones,
Enduring the sea for the dance of the bones.

While the sea practices bones,
With the sea moon known by its bones,
The beach may be quiet from milling its bones,
A figure for sea, and the dance of its bones.

When the sea bones practice the dance,
And black the moon, distant in dance,
Dark are the sea bones, dark is their dance,
Trusting the sea, the moon and their dance.

When the sea bones finish their dance,
Thrown by the sea from the dance,
The beach bears away the bones in the dance,
A figure for haven, for the sake of the sea,
      and for the sake of the sea bones' dance.

In Praise of the Sea

Something is lonely about the sea,
Her long tides and weathers
With no thought of purpose, no repose,
Melancholy, demanding every patience and wit.

The vast void of dream
Is the sea, winding the boat beneath you, you
Who may have the sea's favor, only to be dashed
By her smallest gesture, your fate not noted
Except as circumstance afford, where swell and wane
The sea's waters. It is incomprehensible
That they are not infinite. Yet,
Beyond joy is the loneliness of the sea.

Gill-over-the-ground

What did the skunk kit have in his mouth?
Gill it was gill it was gill-over-the-ground.
Smooth dainty vine grew the yard all around
And clenched he a leaf of gill on his tooth,
Making of sound not a sound.

Who found the skunk kit clutching its leaf?
I it was I knew well where it lay, its belly
      all bloody and sawn.
It was just brief at morning, early first light,
I went darkly,
      darkly at dawn
Sparing my neighbor the odd little grief
Of the small cold form on the lawn.

Who mauled the skunk kit? Calamity's name!
Spirit my greyt hound, Spirit was near.
Alerted she was as we walked in the lane,
      and rapt in the black flame of fear,
jumped at some darkling in dead of the night,
      snapped something wild and untame.
And I knew nothing, I stopped nothing;
      close, so close yet unclear.

In re the ruined kit what is the jury's bill?
Would that a moon's light had shown on the hill!
Moon, Moon, oh why not glow where he fed?
Reveal not the kit? Leave dark as night
      as he grazed in his lasting chill bed?
Wayward late Spirit, dog in my mind,
      Spirit what have you set nil?
And why see I now your drunken sad lurch,
    hear now your harrowing keen,
    have now you coming, coming to me
    loathsome, all loathsome, in red?

It is said that to understand someone,
you must first love him. But once you love him,
It is unnecessary to understand him.
—Roshi Phillip Kapleau

Magic Under

Under my house grow rooms, multiplying by night,
small rooms for my workshops, tiny machines,
    good maple benches,
the lease-out to the car repair with its greasy smells
redolent of my father's trade,
rooms for the people of the house, animal folk, wanderers-in.
I slip past strangers, unknown enterprises,
labor with the sour plumbing, jury-rigged electricals,
the cranky old furnace,
staunch the occasional geyser from the floor.
Some capped-off drains you just don't dare crack open.

Tonight
there is a whole new apartment. Black, black,
they are black, their ivory smiles
covering the distance to the door where I stand,
    at last taken aback
at what my basement does.
Not understood, their patois, explaining, inviting,
except in the dark dignity of rhythms.
I smell the frying plantains as never before,
the cumin beans and chicken,
take a cup of their dark, familiar rum.

The bright bare bulb swinging from its wire—
the starkness of its necessity
and the shadows of its necessity
threaten to overwhelm me.
How to know the grandmother's crushed legs in rags
on the abandoned mattress?
There is a child missing in her smile.

Somewhere they have found wallpaper oddments
and it catches at me, the mishmash wild patterns
    of the roll ends,
recalling the bright carefree pastels and primaries
    of Port Au Prince.
Somehow they have divined the ground where I stand,
theirs having fallen away.

What the Eye Knows

The eye knows its business
knows the cold, disconsolate rains
of April, can acknowledge
their onset in a flicker at the heart.

While my marvelously self-righting butt
and the oft-acclaimed brain
sink back toward the bottom
of some vertigo
as I whirl my car around the exit ramp of I-590,
my eye has scanned the spruces
spinning against my course,
and picked out a lump
just off the apex of one,
something that doesn't belong
And does,

seen the slight gold
of its breast, its large utterly alive stillness
and instantly my eye has whispered
its surpassing poise.

Lacunae

Looming night after night in my headlights' glance,
    why is the raccoon slouching so agonizingly into oblivion,
    its body ruining along the road's berm?
And why would the 'possum lie unmarked,
    unmolested day after day in its field,
    the leaves beneath it larger than those on the tree;
    the tiny snake stiff and cold in its grass, unfed?
Yesterday a circular rainbow gleamed around the horizon
    north nor'east in the clouds,
    followed by a smarting shaft of sunlight
    and a hard, spotty rain.

The night is quiet, its stars silent,
Individually inked out.
Not even blinking aircraft lights,
nor northern auroral curtains,
nor even the city's brilliance
    glows above.
Gone these many weeks, gone.
What has become of the moon?

Cajolery

The skies are ringing with geese,
and in the park at the foot of our road for days now,
weeks early here
on frigid Lake Ontario.

The parklands spread thin
their wintered-over greens and frozen browns,
muddy, poised between warmth and frost.
Precarious as a lost glove spring seems
    in this moment, as I doubt its power.

Looking from my shop window under the cedars' shadows
at the light-stencilled earth
and the bright fallow field beyond,
their seductions tease at my tidy comfort.

In the gray afternoon March rattles its reeds,
dabbles at budding.
Its chilly fingers blow my hair the wrong way,
flaunting ramshackle charms.

II. Home Roads

Nested Dreams and Reasons

Under the bromide streetlight,
    crushed stone lying about the casually filled hole
    might seem to be crabapple blossoms shed in the breeze.
Our neighborhood clutches so at its poor streets,
    its little shrunken yards, the trees that shove
    the house foundations awry.
The eye can't miss the dreams as one walks along.

As a child I couldn't understand why
    the curbing ended where it did,
    twenty yards into Bohannon Street, and why
    gravel was content to lie in the middle
    of some intersections,
    baking in the relentless sun, and why
you could catch crawdads in the ditches
only round where we lived.

For crawdads, the reasons for things
    are always local, and beyond them the crawfish
    hold sway,
    working crawfish sense.
Beyond their claws' reach in this under-fed neighborhood,
    one may walk at peace in the blues and reds
    of day's end,
pondering this place where the tinkering
and machinery in backyards and paved lots
works for a while and then doesn't anymore.

The mice are back in the house.
I'll have to find the tunnel they've chewed
down along the foundations, fill it full of mortar.
We're always killing things, here, inside the reasons
    between dreams.

On Loma Garden

I went searching for Woody's old house on Loma Garden,
    sitting in its little Mimosa-infested yard.
And the Crepe Myrtle had got all out of hand,
    its long naked arms
    silver and brown, waving a clutch of late October blossoms,
    teased me with spring that smelled like my boyhood,
    dusky pecan, sweet grasshopper spittle,
    new-mown grass like watermelon, the living room
    faintly scented of coal oil, the rocks' dusty smell in the road.

Woody's old front porch,
    nothing but a big concrete slab really,
    leans now toward the house,
    a pair of old schoolbus seats,
    some large clay pots of flowers.
Up and down the street, these strangers who are here
    look briefly—
    the skinny girl giving her brother's car a Saturday
    night doll-up,
(She pops out the driver's window and peers over the roof.)
Funny little fox-eared dogs bark and trot up officiously,
    sniffing my ankles and fingers,
The next-door boys stop wrestling and yelping with their dog
    in the dusk of their front yard. Their mamma in the house
    continues to fold clothes, their father out back,
    mowing the field
    where the old wreck lies up cock-eyed on blocks
—They all look, their eyes blank with interest.

The gravel, Texas pea gravel, in the road looks old, old
    as if it had been tamped into a stream-filtered bed
    where it lay the ages long.
Things happen so simply there is no past left.
The hours and afternoons die instantly,
leaving of memory only small stones.

Down the street, two girls spend the Saturday nightfall
    in the porch swing, talking in whoops
    about their boyfriends' missteps and promises.
Boyhood smells, the smell of the smothering sameness
    of Saturday afternoons,
    little hair bits down your shirt from sweaty, oiled haircuts.
    the barber's cologne, tame man-smell
    slapped on your neck and ears,
the smell of a slow, sturdy poverty
that I owned once and knew,
now occupied by strangers
with their own dogs and boys.

Daddy's Passing

After the stroke my dad's false teeth
    shared his mouth
    like vagrants while he talked.
As I roared delightedly
    he would jumble out something
    while his teeth clapped their own notion.

Great lightening slit the room
    through the Venetian blinds,
    rebounding to no apparent effect
    among the hospital furniture.

Outside, thunder brought the dawn
    but dawn was dry, gray, with a skinny thought
    of glory at the sun.
The air conditioning equipment
    populating the roof outside the window
    stood like toys, in mimicry
    of the solemn cedars perched on the chalk cliffs
    where Scyene Road twists and turns its way
    like an old man on an errand.

He lay in bed and I sliced turnips for our breakfast,
    peppermint candy and crackers, cauliflower, grapes,
    which we ate as we joked, his face clear as a drink of water
    rinsed with pain.

After we had eaten and the grey sky was complete,
    came the rain,
    bald, parsimonious.
On that morning of hard thin rain and rumbling thunder,
    looking at me with the astonishment of a captured hawk,
    he declared between his roaming teeth,
    Before Jesus takes you, ye must suffer!
    and asked would I meet him in Paradise.

That day he began refusing all help, even asleep,
    spat his pills furiously,
    demanding, *Peppermint!*

He prayed grievously to enter Glory,
    and Jesus took him later, by night,
    as the cedars stood at attention on the chalk
    behind the hospital,
As befits the passing of the saints.

Up Drop Jaw Hill

Winston, eyeing every rock and ledge,
    puts the wheels on them one by one
    bucking his pickup strong aslant
Up Drop Jaw Hill
    past the charnel yard,
    a golgotha of wild boar offal,
    past the deer baits,
    past the hunters' blinds,

Up onto the hill's shattered cap
    limestone, half-marble, chert,
    gnarled cedar racks, thousands,
Caught in the desert halfway between life and death,
    under the ocean sky.

Here it's too steep and we get out,
    climb in the cicadas' skirling tinnitus
    onto Drop Jaw's ridge, where life and death
    are not so admixed,
    where rock is pure, views pristine,
    like an old commentary that roars through
    our harsh history,
Needing no more words.

A little more than a year
    our sister had laid in the ground
    and I'd found many meditations
    on how life and death intertwine, ranting at the one
    for being so like the other.

And now on Drop Jaw Hill
    we gingerly pick our way around each other's path
    respectful with our words
    of old animosities
    differences, mistakes
And appreciative each of the other
    how he uses his staff
    his own damn way, and at last,
Bittersweet, I find playfulness again.

We explore until exhausted
the trail's twists and marches,
marvel, brotherly heads together,
over finding hard blood-red seeds up here,
knapped chert,
    cast-off antlers
Among the valiant wind-burnished cedars.

Back at camp we drink cold beer, watching
    as the children living here alone
        laugh, cook in the kitchen trailer, hold their own school,
        playing late in the campfire evening,
Growing up artlessly at the foot of Drop Jaw Hill.

Labor Day

I have seen the American folk taken as a cruel harvest
Seen them mowed from their roots and craft
Seen them bagged like leaves, like shredded secrets,
    collected on the empty fields of their own homes,
    bulldozed by mortgages and Urban Renewal
    into landfills
    and capped with an impervious clay of official policy.

I have seen them in the fish markets of Capitalism, Globalism,
    trying to flip back into the ocean of their labor —
    now far away —
    craftspeople, secretaries, engineers, factory workers,
    aircraft fabricators, software programmers, farmers
    sent slithering into the holding pens
    of unnecessary prey,
    their jobs obliterated or taken overseas
    to those glad for the dimes.
Seen them pacing streets, left with pocket change,
    begging at intersections to work for food,
    given programs run from surplus desks in
    abandoned buildings
    by begrudging bureaucrats.
Seen their energy distracted, their contrariness broken,
    their native work hobbled, their creativity
    managed to death.
Seen the knowing nods and companionable sympathy
    from war veterans and welfare moms —
    been there, still doing that, crazy with it.

I have seen the American folk like plains of wheat,
    gathered from over the Earth
    enriching the vision and courage of the land.
Seen them scythed in a fell salvation
    by preachers called, they say, by Jesus
    to the seat of American power from now 'til Armageddon,
    the obedient to be swept up in Rapture,

  knowers of Truth,
  baiters of men, women, blacks,
  baiters of Muslims, Jews, trade unionists,
  baiters of lesbos, queers and other wildlife,
  dividing & twisting,
  dividing & twisting,
  until one skein doesn't know its sisters and brothers
  the next skein over, though shoulder to shoulder they be.

I have seen them derided for not giving their children to war,
  while the evangelists of American empire
  quietly hide their own,
Seen their sons and daughters answer the call of duty
  or get drafted or dodge the draft
  sent to hold the checkpoints of American hegemony,
  battling for everything back home
  against people standing in their own homes.
Seen them come back alone, unblessed,
  mangled, sometimes mocked,
  spat on by pacifists,
  covered in the ironic excrement of war's glory.

Seen them insulted for knowing that, for paying
  too much attention,
  for not paying enough attention,
  for not shopping, for owing too much,
  for being fat, for being scrawny.
Seen them insulted for having sex and poverty
  and children and sorrow instead of loneliness
  — then having the loneliness after all
  for having sex when you don't want babies,
  for needing an abortion even though you abhor abortions.
Seen them insulted for living too long, for not
  being old enough
  for voting while black, while poor,
  for being too black, not black enough.

Seen them insulted for being too smart, too dumb,
    too lost, too saved,
    too punked out, too goth,
    profiled likely to be packing heat at school.

I have seen the American folk chumped by admen,
    salesmen, pitchmen, spammers, public relations hucksters,
    cooing celebs certain you'll want their lipstick,
    growled at to buy pickup trucks or
    luxury combat vehicles to drive under the sparkling sun
    through your maple-shady life.
Buy yer drugs, getcher doc to prescribe 'em (or not).
Buy stocks, buy bonds, buy a gun — two, three —
    Belligerence Is Your American Right.
Drink beer lotsa beer, drink Pepsi, drink Coke, drink
Cranapple —
    drink *something* for chrissakes.
Shave your face, shave your legs, shave your ass,
    wax your crotch.
Buy pretty perfume
    buy your dreams
    buy your life.
Be sexy.
Be powerful with remote control
    in the blue glamour of your TV.

I have seen us fist-fighting in street clothes on Jerry Springer.
Seen us dying of news poisoning,
    our wan faces considering the phony voices
    blasting out of the televisions bolted to the ceiling.
Seen us drowning in the blood of innocents we have bombed
    all the way into Jeffersonian Democracy
    then all the way back out again.
Seen us drowning in the CIA's assassinations.

Our own butlers of terror day after day drowning us
    at the School of the Americas,
    at Gitmo, at Abu Graib,
    at who knows where.
Seen us choked with the effort to speak
    what our bones know
    as we hang by our tongues from America.

We cry out for one!
We cry out for one who will convene the American folk
Away from dreams of empire
Away from wars of adventure
Away from foreign policy made of explosions,
    poisons and fear.

We cry out for one who will convene the American folk
To belong to the American land.
We are its forests
We are its rivers
We are its cities and towns, the scintillating life of its streets
We, the lakes on its breast
We, the long marches of its prairie
We are the obdurate activity of its mountains,
    the black obsidian of their deep fire.
We are its heart, its mind.
Our thoughts, our dreams,
Our hopes for our kin and our folk, for our nation, for its soil
Are none other than this American continent,
Its aspirations, its long meditation.
Our lives are the tides of its dream.

IV. Learning to Die

The Turtle of Running

The turtle of pain, lying at ease
    on the sandbar, stirs itself
    in order to achieve a higher state,
    ideas being no fit companion
while my feet slap the painful pavement. Ideas
    are there to make you wish
you didn't hurt, to remind you
    of the difference.

Not caring for such tear-sucking dragonflies,
    the turtle of pain blinks them away and
    moves just enough to concentrate
    better on the sand
    that is always there, is always
moving away from under you,
    always muddy when you are dry,
    gritty when you are wet.

The turtle of pain, not being squeamish
    concerning anguish and sloth, turns on
    the sand to get the sun full on its back,
    and does not concentrate,
does not think of iced tea
    or peaches, or of lactic acid
groaning in my hips and legs,

running to somehow here, where
now is somehow this.

Heat

Heat lay like a gentling,
    and the flickering shade of trees caressed
    my iridescent skin
    like a satin gown brushing against my legs, and

The summer noon its sun
    beating on all the indefensible sidewalks,
    the abandoned doorways,
on the abused street itself, blue in its obeisance,
    blanching whatever
    dare its gaze,
lay on me as tantalizing silks.

My hard hot panting a stroke of lace
    running into it I ran into it the heat, clothed
shamelessly transvestite in July,
    in its embrace,
    there being no surcease,
bottomless the moment, given
in the gentling hand of July.

Learning to Die in May

The actual blood, potential
    in the veins everywhere beneath the skin,
    coursing in every organ,
    perfusing even her thought,
    was itself a labyrinth of ideas
    until it coughed up surprised at the sheets.

The awareness that was the blood
    had no specific seat—
    we knew only that the bony vaults were no more
    than an eventual residence, one among many,
    of her flickering clarity.

The momentary eye lay in its socket so surprised
    at the light,
    at its ability to blink,
    startled that one might come
    to this nether reach of life
    and not know how to die.

And around the mother swirled
    the gentle stew of household living,
    the half-conscious certitudes and embarrassments
    of a family who expects to outlast tomorrow.
We did not know we did not know how to die.
It is not a matter of flow,
    curiosity cannot winkle it out,
    nor can you learn it
    as you might a taste
    for green olives.

The cats and dogs of the city
    might know, in a weak moment—
    tired or scared perhaps—
    or maybe taken with a notion of happiness,
    might with a strayed mind choose
    to be some idea of blood
    or an utterly plausible beauty.

They might for instance fall in love
> during the smell of mown grass,
> or have a way of clawing a hole
> in the ground so a house might be fitted into it,
> and thus acquire a glimmer
> of death's necessity.

II

There is a universe, a void of mind
> yearning, it would seem, for knowing,
> to have some bony vault in which
> to live for instance,
> blinking through sockets, the smooth
> cheeks (built for holding nuts or gobbets of flesh)
> concealing the ancient grin
> of high form.

But even in such a mansion, for one
> given to thought,
> intimations of impermanence arouse
> ideas of mortality as if death
> were something one knows or does
> or must know how to do.

And thus must choose
> or not.

And thus even the mice of the house
> may seem optional,
> their necessity missed or mistaken
> for effect or cause,
> as if we knew what they are for,
> or as if we knew why cats and dogs
> like the crunch of their bones.

We might go so far in the pleasant gray
> dreariness of May afternoons
> as to ponder them, models of their demise,
> blessing them for the lesson in death.

But the blood coursing
    in even such veins is not of this,
    is not anything of our kenning,
    as it winks through
    the tiny ultimates of the circulation
    we know they must have.
And though we can prove the necessity
    of such inferences by the
    serial and simultaneous dissections
    of sufficient mice
    (each one as alive under a scalpel as may ever be),
There is nothing
    nothing that can be inferred about any
    or every mouse, nor about the mortal business
    of muggy afternoons of May,

Except that our temptation to do so,
the yearning that is beyond
notions of power or knowledge or happiness,
is a piece of the world.
The yearning to know of death
is a piece of the world
just like the mice.

Your Mother's Last Breath

Your mother's last breath smells of her milk,
    the slightly rancid sweetness of it drying on your bib.
    Pungent, somewhat sour the smell of her body
    as she lies in her last hour, without affect
    other than a sigh and the pulse at her throat.

Her last breath taunts you with the smells of her kitchen,
    cinnamon, black-eyed peas, fish, cornbread,
    underlain by the smell of her body,
    soon, now, to be claimed
by forces she has always danced with,
    a few times mastering, sometimes herself overcome.

As you breathe in this lurid perfume
    in the presence of her unlidded eyes,
    her lips slack, tongue unmoving,
your mother's last breath fills a moment
    in which all your words, all your thoughts,
    all your wishes, all distractions
are brought to a stop
before her unfathomable ability to be there
    and then not.

She will pass easily from this moment.
But how shall you?

Mother's Day

It may have been a wondrous work
to bare the flesh against the cheek
to secret through the tiny lips
all her humors, all her hopes
    secret humors in her hopes.

It may have called for doughty hope
to lay a home when home itself was hardly known
to pray for help, to pray for prayer
to know of dark and shrieking pain
    shrieking darkness all unknown.

It may have started all of cries
all of tenderly met loss
pious dread and dismal doubt
to follow yearnings all to bed
in gentle darkness take the load
    unrequited load, all of faith.

It may have shaken, down the years,
soul by roots, dire presentiments of loss and more
witnessing the fading limbs
one by one, careering off to life or worse
muster time and time again in smaller world
    smaller world yet full, some full.

It may have been the gift in darkness,
tried the years of durable pain, yet from the first
accorded to the suckling need,
that joined her soul
that dreamed a dream
    unknown dream than ever could she dream.

Last. or Maybe First

Where there is no jam, no butter, no toast
no fine morning glistening like a raw egg in the sky
where there is no everyday clean shirt and socks
project done, job done

Where there is no goodbye, hello,
love you too, come back soon
where coming home, leaving home, staying home
are no longer adventures

Where there is no honing the sensibilities,
    self help books gone to Goodwill
no more temper tantrums, no hankering for chocolate
no New Year's Resolutions
no searching for the truth, God or The Eternal Principle

Where all that can be undone and done, repented and said
has been undone and done, repented and said
where you've come to terms, somehow, with your pain
where your life is no longer a drama

Who are you there, what are you,
my fine crafter of ideas, visions and words,
what of all the grasping at making
that hand and habit need?

Let go that too, even that,
moment by moment by moment?
Eternity, you know, is very ordinary—
just like right now.

My Hair

My hair gets so excited when I sleep.
Its grey feckless whorls
    cringe from the comb,
    and leap for its brothers, my eyebrows,
Its hoary sisters the tufts
    on the edges of my ears.

My hair senses, in its own way, how
    I hate the neighbor's spotlight
    steadfast at our bedroom window,
    making sure we don't burgle his kitchen.
It misses the quiet starry nights
    of Pleasant Grove where you could see
    the Milky Way, where you could smell thunder
    miles away in the dark,
    see its dusky flash
    on the horizon.

Now it has nothing to feed its enthusiasms
    except dreams.
    Mostly these days, I tire myself out working in
    my little shop.
    My hair should approve of that.
One night I woke up sore afraid, as they say,
    a dark shape looming in the hall. If I'd had
    a pistol my daughter
    would have died with her bladder still full,
    so I'm against the NRA.

I don't understand the night anymore.
Or my hair.

Dokusan

In the morning sometimes, fleshless tears
Well up. The bones of some old karma
Heaved from the grave by a new frost.

It is then the beginner's mind will hear
The floors (sound as ever) moan
At the step of some inobtrusive buddha
Preparing the way.

And it is then,
The hammer testing the hand,
Bell!

Unfinished Song
In memory of our first greyhound, Raku

The day Raku died I thought the giant sky in me
Would flare like some sea anemone
Opening on the wildness of his world.

The day Raku died I thought the small blue flowers
 dancing in the grass
Would speak to me at last, would be my mind,
No longer just some random grace of May.

The day Raku died I thought his slipping off to dust
 would break my heart,
Let all the blood and poetry go murmuring into streams,
When he fixed his eye on the wilderness of death.

Grief's Terrain

Sometimes I wonder
    at how she sings in my mind
    Sinatra tunes, church hymns, ad jingles,
    pouring through me
In her young voice,
    so present, so deeply moving,
Yet now from a country so far
    it seems a strange grieving,
    though well I know this realm.

Chanting for her
    with some compassionate friend,
    my voice becomes tearful
Like a damaged cannon,
    its force unaimed and blurting,
    yet thus coupling my efforts to hers
    as she traverses that abysmal terrain.

Or simply sitting alone,
    pleading in silence for bodhisattvas' aid
    in her journey through that unlit land.
I know that place of haunts, somehow familiar,
    as firmly as I know my unvoiced chant.
Firmly as the dream

On my pillow, where I lie alone too long
    abed in the morning nursing pain,
    a rib broken just days before she died,
As if suffering again Adam's sleep
    while Jehovah slowly shoves the rib back in,
    claiming back to Himself the first woman,
of whose body I came,
    who made from herself my ribs,
    for whom I now light the way
    with chant and song and grieving
    through death's domain.

Night Emergencies

The screamed *Why??*
Rose to an ultimate ululation
Beating on the door of the lockup
After hours of sobbing and moans,
Emerging as the cry of the loon,
Amid the placid cacophony of bleeps and bings,
A nocturne of electronic crickets, katydids, tree peepers,
Stalk-eyed robots emitting vital signs.

Below these thrummed the night polisher,
Following its approach/avoidance scheme,
Through the aisles' pattern.

And overrunning all this,
As a surf will spend the night
On a shelving beach,
Pounded deep mortal pain,
Asking no quarter except the mercy
Of being left alone with grief.

V. You're Becoming a Song

Dreams with Katherine

I awaken to moonlight under snow
Bathing the room.
You have forgotten your rings,
And they glint in the pearly shadow,
Small and sturdy as promises
From there where I clasp your hand
In the frosted night.

A Small House

A small house makes a magic home,
    being, as it must, larger on the inside
    than out. Yet for all its wonders
    its limitations impose,
    or suggest, necessities, disciplines.

Similarly, those inhabiting a small house
    must be larger inside than out,
    ready for connections with all who are there
    without the least suggestion of cobwebs
    or bad electricity or sour plumbing.

Householding can be peculiar.
There may be no places
    for closeting, for instance, or for make-up,
    glue, hammer,
    the odd inflammable.

Belongings should be as sparse, of course,
    as harsh words. Loud expressions or feelings
    may find little projection
    in a small house,
Or may rattle it apart if persistent.

Living in a small house is a jewel to be glimpsed,
    perhaps turned from time to time,
    but never stared at.
To census-takers wanting the exact number of occupants,
    reply there is no such figure.
Never, never measure the foundations.

Regarding Roselle's Buddha,

whose pastel face arises from its white paper
like ribbons riding a breeze

Or the colors of an oil film
floating elaborately on the tide

Between dream
and dream.

Margaret Cried So, Our Last Night

Go your way. Or stay a moment longer,
    stand here and look through this window.
The time to leave sits over there, knees tight
against its chest,
        in that clammy comfortable chair.

Wind jerks and sneezes, brushes across the yard
   sighs, rains
   and sighs

Stand here and wait to stay or fiddle with leaving.
Dumbly wait fidgety for a May shower.
Hold even our nasty tempered ill-timed time
    over there; in that corner;
    so. And let us dwell earnestly before the
        demand

of a sighing cupful of rain now and again
    tossed gently across the yard.

Eve On Her Hill

Eve on her hill in the clover,
collar pulled against an autumn chill.
The first tart wind of winter
furrowed her brow like a new love
as I slipped words down her breasts.

Eve on her hill
pink on the snow
pulling me over her like blankets,
her breath tasting of flowers
while the clouds rushed at the cornfield.

Eve on her hill
heavy with children
smelling of milk gone and milk yet to be,
her skirts snapping away from her like flags
in the wind easting at the corn.

You're Becoming a Song

    You're becoming a song
    That my arms think is true.
    My arms think they hold you,
    Where they think you belong.
    You're becoming the song I make
    As the day moves along.
    But somewhere you're alive, awake!
    And there, my song's just a song.

In the first lighting of a dawn, my mind's knowing you,
Nuzzling in your dark waves of hair, and there at your ear
Whispering something you'd never know,
    while dreaming's still true,
I wake now to find that you are still miles, miles from here.

    My arms think they hold you,
    Where they think you belong.

I wake and go up the stairs, somewhere you're rising too,
We take our accustomed seats beyond the day's empty power,
Dwell in wonderful silences, plumbing mind
    through and through;
I feel your warmth on the air, as we rise from that hour.

    You're becoming the song I make
    As the the day moves along

Rising under the lowering sky, the sun burns off the gloom,
Then gaining above the clouds, all shadows are gone.
Sipping out of my coffee cup, I move 'round the room,
Then my mind tries to chase your hand onto your telephone.

The difference between my mind and having you here,
Finding no presence real and live, just your warmth on the air,

Is excitement, is all I have, but I bend it 'til fair,
Slowly changing my mind to song that cherishes you.

> You're becoming a song
> That my arms think is true.
> My arms think they hold you,
> Where they think you belong.
> You're becoming the song I make
> As the the day moves along.
> But somewhere you're alive, awake!
> And there, my song's just a song.

Sassafras
(after reading John Keats "Bright Star")

I've found in the meadow across the lane
    A hundred golden deaths,
Devotion's tokens
    For Katherine, last and true

And thought of John,
    Who wished for nothing
Than lie on Fanny's tender breast,
    Yet walked amid his forlorn hope
So gently into that good night.

And walk I here, sunlit
    In showered vows,
In death of life ever to come,
    This path I wish were also his,
Bowered so gently
    In long years' tender troth.

Now 'cross the years from dismal fate,
    Fervent wish fulfilled
In such a small and fleeting coin,
    John's fletched my own desire
With such sweet harmonies

These currencies to weave
    For an arrow path
Fair Katherine I bid to tread,
And settle sweetly on a throne
    Full golden in sassafras.

Eve Gives Lavender

With a stave of lavender
she broke in and stole my peace.
It took the rest of the day
to put an end to her.

VI. Dulcimer Verses

Frog

The frog croaks
out of nowhere
its green eye
a hole in the world.

Night Geese

Geese are haunting the sky tonight,
their fingers splayed on the darkness
like a skater breaking a fall.
Now and then
one cuts the ray of a star
or cries out to its neighbors
a call I barely resist.

First Love

First love
Then joy
And then silence.
Then *music*.

Coffee

Looking in dreams
for a gloss on the day,
we swaddle ourselves
in the remnants of sleep,
stranded past night
like ghosts, clinging
to the steamy comforts of
coffee in bed.

The Bell

Reality's bell is made of irony;
strike it hard if you require that matters be clear
caress, if it's music you want.

The Use of Crying

Drink your tears;
If they are sweet, know impermanence
If they are bitter, know suffering
If they are sour, know remorse
If they are salt,
Know the Earth that supports you in Great Emptiness.

Willow

In the bitterly pure snow outside my window,
old pussywillow, sure of what I only hope,
quietly greens her buds.

Dukkha

Creation's joy is written
On the parchment of sorrow.

Ghosts

July's morning heat was still young
when the dog's toenails,
sauntering across the pavement,
evaporated every ghost except
the squalid purity of the street.

Night Song

Sometimes the winter wind
regales the pine tops with its somber hymns,
and the tree trunks rub their own woody song,
fluting and bassooning at one another
up the hillside behind our house,
like whales serenading
in the snowy gray ocean of night.

Canon

Today the dogs and I
hiked the Hojak Trail
with cicadas who thrilled
throughout the broad simple day
some cyclic secret
utterly beyond my ken.

Autumn

Tatterdemalion on the sky,
wild clouds frisk me
with fiery shadows
new endings, old beginnings
autumn's sweet bitters.

Moon

Why does the loon cry in the night,
the finger point out the moon?
Gird not yourself against her tides
pulling at the water of you.

Me

Against the snow fence last summer's leaves
wrappers from the corner deli
the snow of every today
the habit of being myself.

Wolf's Moon

When the wolf sits
beneath the bitter moon
forgo your warmth.
taste for an hour her night.

Spring Vigil

I awoke deep in the night and lay attending
to the chorus of frogs
and the dusty perfume of the coming rain.

Samadhi

Where the mind is silent a moment
it may suddenly soar off its usual nest
into joy.

April

Chilly April eve,
    its moonlight crazed
    by the bare trees,
pregnant with the chorus of frogs
scrubbing the night clear.